ZEE GROWS A TREE

Elizabeth Rusch

illustrated by

Will Hillenbrand

CANDLEWICK PRESS

One spring morning, little Zee Cooper arrived in the world.

The very same day, a Douglas-fir seedling emerged from the soil at Coopers' Christmas Tree Farm.

In the wild, Douglas-fir seeds need cold and moisture to trigger their growth. At a nursery, farmers wet and cool the seeds, then plant them in warm soil to help get them ready to grow.

For the first months of Zee's life, her mom and
dad cared for her every day and night, feeding her,
burping her, and changing her diaper.

Zee's mom and dad cared for her little tree, too,
feeding it, watering it, and pulling the weeds.
Together, Zee and her tree grew bigger and stronger.

Farm-raised Douglas-firs live their first few years
sheltered in a nursery, where they are protected from
insects, animals, and diseases that threaten seedlings
in the wild.

Zee's Tree

After just a few years, Zee was ready to start preschool—and her tree was ready to start life outside the nursery.

Zee's Tree

At school, Zee made new friends and learned her ABC's.

In the field, her tree met new critters and experienced how the weather changed from day to day. Zee took good care of her tree, and its roots stretched deep into the ground.

In the first years of a Douglas-fir's life, most of the changes happen underground, in the roots, which spread down and outward to absorb water and nutrients.

On Zee's fourth birthday, her father marked her height on the kitchen doorway. Zee was shorter than the other kids in her class. "Don't worry," her father said. "Everyone grows at different rates."

Zee measured her tree's height. It was also smaller than the others. She stroked the whorls of branches—there were four whorls in total, one for each year. "Don't worry," she said. "Everyone grows at different rates."

Humans grow fast for the first few years, after which their rate of growth slows. Douglas-fir trees tend to grow faster and faster each year.

Many evergreen trees do most of their growing for the year in spring to early summer. Douglas-firs typically grow from April through July.

When summer arrived, Zee outgrew all her clothes. Zee's
tree grew, too, reaching a foot higher in just one month!
Zee's tree was finally taller than she was!

The following fall, when Zee started kindergarten, she got a whole new look.

Her tree was looking pretty spiffy, too.

In the wild, Douglas-firs can grow into irregular shapes with bare patches and some bent or bushy branches. To get a perfect cone shape, farmers prune the top and shear the sides.

In first grade, Zee learned all kinds of exciting new things: how to add big numbers, how to draw a castle, and how to juggle a soccer ball.

"Look at me!" she said to her tree.

When a heavy bird snapped off the top of Zee's tree, the tree learned something new, too—how to turn a branch into a new treetop!

When the top of a Douglas-fir tree is missing—because it breaks or has been trimmed off—another branch grows up toward the sky to become the new top. This branch is called "the leader."

In second grade, Zee lost three teeth, one right after the other. A few weeks later, three new teeth poked through her gums.

In May, new buds burst forth at the top of Zee's tree and started growing branches.

Unlike people, whose entire bodies lengthen when they grow, Douglas-fir trees lengthen only from the top and roots.

Later that spring, it got hot. Really, really hot. It was the hottest, driest spring anyone could remember.

Zee noticed that her tree looked pale with thin, scraggly branches. She studied her tree up close. Big patches of needles had turned dry and brown. "You don't feel well, do you?" she said, stroking the brittle branches.

Zee grabbed a watering can and poured water around the parched tree. She fanned it and spread ice cubes on the ground around its trunk. "It's the heat," Zee whispered. "Don't worry, I'll take care of you."

If a heat wave or drought hits in the spring, Douglas-firs can suffer from heat stress, which dries and darkens their needles. There is no treatment, but most trees recover.

Douglas-firs on farms are usually not watered. Like trees in the wild, they depend on rain. But during a severe drought, some farmers take extra measures to get water to their plants.

During the summer, Zee lugged water to her tree every week. She camped beside it whenever she could. She even shared her freezer pops.

Zee did everything she could to protect her tree in its
weakened state. In the fall, she heaped mulch at its base to
keep the ground warm and moist.

In the winter, she constructed a burlap screen to protect its branches from icy breezes.

Douglas-firs enter a period of inactivity in the winter called dormancy. Though they can get quite cold, sugars and other substances in their cells keep them from freezing. But harsh winter winds can cause the needles to dry out and suffer from windburn.

That spring, Zee celebrated her eighth birthday by unwrapping the burlap from her tree. It was still shorter and scragglier than the other trees, but it stood strong. "You made it," she whispered.

Zee fed her tree. As the weeks passed, the tree grew and grew—and turned a deep, rich green. She caressed its soft new needles. "You're getting healthier every day!" she said.

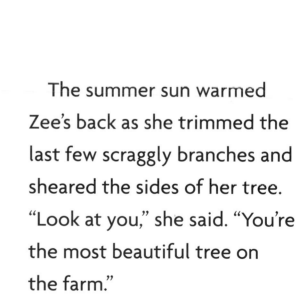

The summer sun warmed Zee's back as she trimmed the last few scraggly branches and sheared the sides of her tree. "Look at you," she said. "You're the most beautiful tree on the farm."

All trees, especially those fighting disease, drought, or insect infestation, need nutrients such as nitrogen, calcium, and potassium. Douglas-firs in the wild must use whatever is available in the soil. Farmers can add nutrients to make sure their trees thrive.

That winter, Zee's tree was finally old enough and tall
enough to become a holiday tree . . .

24

After seven or eight years, a Douglas-fir reaches between six and eight feet tall, the perfect height for most Christmas trees.

An uncut Douglas-fir can live for hundreds of years and grow to be more than three hundred feet tall!

26

And Zee was old enough
and tall enough to decorate
it herself, all the way to the top.

INDEX

Look up the pages to find out about all these tree things.

Don't forget to look at both kinds of words—**this kind** and this kind.

LONG LIVE THE TREE!

While cut trees are not bad for the environment (most tree farms plant two trees for every one that is cut), you can also enjoy a holiday tree without having to cut one down.

A tree planted outside your home can be decorated year-round with ornaments or homemade decorations, or with strings of popcorn and cranberries to feed the birds.

Trees can also be dug up and brought into the house for holidays, then left in a large pot outside or replanted in your yard.

If you want to bring a tree in for winter holidays, move it indoors gradually over a few days so that it doesn't get too warm too fast. Start the potted tree in your garage or basement. When you move it inside, choose a cool room away from heat. (If the tree gets too warm, it will think it's spring and will begin to grow!) Water the tree only enough to keep its roots from drying. Dump ice cubes into the planter once in a while to remind the tree that it's winter.

You can keep the tree indoors for about a week or so. Then move it to increasingly cooler spots in your home, and finally place the container outside until the next holiday. Or plant the tree in your yard to enjoy it for the rest of your life!

FURTHER READING

Burns, Diane. *Trees, Leaves, and Bark.* Minocqua, WI: NorthWord, 1995.

Green, Jen. *The Magic and Mystery of Trees.* New York: DK, 2019.

Hickman, Pamela. *Nature All Around: Trees.* Toronto: Kids Can Press, 2019.

Ingoglia, Gina. *The Tree Book: For Kids and Their Grown-Ups.* New York: Brooklyn Botanic Garden, 2008.

Purmell, Ann. *Christmas Tree Farm.* New York: Holiday House, 2006.

To Izzi and all the living things she loves
ER

For all who love our precious earth, seeking and acting
on hope hidden in a pine cone, starting with a seemingly
simple seed—the promise of new life
WH

First edition 2021

Library of Congress Catalog Card Number 2021933615
ISBN 978-0-7636-9754-9

22 23 24 25 TLF 10 9 8 7 6 5 4 3 2

Printed in Dongguan, Guangdong, China

This book was typeset in Agenda.
The illustrations were done in mixed media.

Candlewick Press
99 Dover Street
Somerville, Massachusetts 02144

www.candlewick.com

IN APPRECIATION

Much
thanks to
Chal Landgren,
a Christmas-tree
specialist and professor
at Oregon State University
and author of *Developing Quality
Christmas Trees in the Pacific
Northwest*, for sharing his extensive
knowledge about
Christmas-tree farming and for the fascinating
tour of the Landgren family farm in Warren,
Oregon. I am also grateful to Hoyt Arboretum plant
taxonomist Mandy Tu for her
additional review of the manuscript for accuracy. Everything
I got right is thanks to Chal and Mandy;
any errors are mine. Thanks also to Elizabeth Goss, Melissa Dalton,
and Erika Schnatz for their research and editing
efforts, and to Addie Boswell, Ruth Feldman, Ellen Howard, Barbara Kerley,
Amber Keyser, Michelle McCann, Sabina Rascol, Mary Rehmann,
Sara Ryan, Nicole Schreiber, and Emily Whitman for their insightful comments.
To my editor, Kaylan Adair, it's been wonderful to grow
and reach milestones with you. My deep appreciation to Will Hillenbrand
for bringing this child and her tree to life. Finally, thanks to Izzi Rusch and her outdoor
evergreen tree, Chris,
for inspiring this story.